MY OWN RAINBOW

Deb McCarthy

BookLeaf
Publishing

India | USA | UK

Presentation by *BookLeaf Publishing*

Web: www.bookleafpub.com

E-mail: info@bookleafpub.com

ISBN: 9789358317145

First edition 2023

DEDICATION

To Dana and James, with much gratitude and love; and to Lisa for keeping me sane by allowing me to talk about things that I can't even write about. I love you all, my friends.

Deb M

To my beautiful children and their families, thank you for everything! I love you more than I can say. xxx

ACKNOWLEDGEMENT

Dana got me back into writing after a long break. She, along with James, gave me encouragement and inspiration, and the courage to say things I hadn't been able to say before.

The most special thanks go to Steph and Jaci for seeing me through myriad trials and tribulations throughout the years and for allowing me to be their Mum. xxx

PREFACE

I write as therapy, to help rid myself of black memories that still haunt, and to hopefully help others who are dealing with their own black memories. I also write to cheer up myself, and hopefully others, with the more lighthearted and fantasy poems. I take inspiration from so many people, places and events, and I'm truly grateful for every bit that I receive.

CUDDLES

Cuddles was a beautiful cat,
Sweet natured and undemanding – for a feline.
For sixteen years our family was blessed
By her presence, her elegant way of moving,
And, when her dignity allowed, the occasional
cuddle.

In winter she'd curl up in front of the fire
As the family gathered around the television.
In the warmer weather
She'd make herself comfortable
On the old wooden garden seat,
Not minding the peeling red pain
Or the noisy children playing in the yard.

Soxy, the black bitsa mutt with four white paws,
Would occasionally bother her,
But one swift swipe of her sharp claws
Would quickly be followed by canine sulking
And skulking away to his purpled kennel
Beneath the wide-spread jacaranda tree.
Cuddles would then stretch luxuriously and
resettle herself
As if the rest of us didn't exist,
Or at least didn't matter.

My Mum said that Cuddles was a tortoiseshell
cat
And my brother called her splotchy,
But to me, in all her feline glory,
She looked like dappled sunlight
On a pile of autumn leaves.

NO PROMISES

He made no promises
She had no expectations
And so when he left
There were no recriminations
Once again a lover
Had played the game
But broke no promises
Always the same
She was the fool
Who let them in
And promise her nothing
Then admit no sin
She lost the game
Each time she played
No promises broken
Just her heart flayed
Now finally
She's had quite enough
It's time for her
To start playing rough
She's found a new man
But no promises she'll make
She's turned hard as nails
It's his heart she'll rake
She'll move onto another

Then keep finding more
In a futile attempt
To even the score
Not realising
That now each new he
Is a gentle person
Like she used to be
Then she finds herself empty
A soul who's bereft
Unable now to care that life
Has no promises left.

VOTE

Let us be subversive and educate the throng;
Divest them of the lies that make their thinking
wrong.
So many people believe that their vote just
doesn't count,
That it won't make any difference to the final
amount.

But this is where they falter; their thinking's all
awry,
For every vote's important to the candidates, no
lie!
Is there no politician who's worth the time it'll
take
To fill out a ballot paper for their country's sake?

Could it be complacency or just pigheadedness?
Do they believe the lies that they oft read in the
press?
"This Seat is a sure thing, for one party or the
other."
Does this "forgone conclusion" mean that no
one has to bother?

Suffrage is a human right, it's the people's
sovereignty;
But many seem to forget that it's also a
responsibility.
For millions this was hard fought for, they
struggled for the right;
A long and bloody battle if they weren't male
and white.

I love that in Australia it's actually a crime
To not uphold one's duty to vote at election time.
But not all countries have this law, and it is such
a shame
That people can't be bothered, so results are
often lame.

Do you look at the outcome and wonder "Did
they fake it?"
Do you have the right to vote but then refuse to
take it?
Are you the ones who lay all blame straight on
the government's plate,
Yet when it come to Election Day, you don't
participate?

You armchair commentators who hate each little
glitch,
Who don't make any effort but like to sit and
bitch,

When the next election's on put down your
damn remote,
Then get up off your asses and go out there and
vote!

A HEALING KIND OF LOVE

"What's the secret to your love?"
A young man asked his Grandma
Ten years after she married the man
He now considered his Grandpa.
"You always seem so happy,
No matter what you go through.
You come from pasts so full of pain
Yet still smile, both of you."

His Grandma took him by the hand
And looked him in the eye.
"It isn't always easy, pet,
But we both always try.
We each were treated badly by
The ones we'd loved before,
But now choose not to accept
That kind of treatment anymore.

"Yet neither of us wants to be
The kind that causes pain,
So treating each other with respect
Keeps us happy, and sane.
The world would be a better place
If this truth we could sell:

'The key to good relationships is
To treat each other well.'

"No love will ever be perfect
For we're humans after all,
But taking your loved one for granted
Is an act that makes you small.
We've had that happen to us
And it gave us broken hearts,
So Grandpa and I work every day
To play true loving parts.

"It shouldn't be a secret,
How love can last so long.
Everyone should be aware of
How to not go wrong.
Yes, both of us had baggage
When we met each other, for sure,
But we help to heal each other's wounds,
Instead of causing more."

MISSED ME SO MUCH

A trauma here, a trauma there,
Trauma, trauma everywhere.
From pedophiles to Mama's dead,
Abused by my ex; I lived in dread.
Admittance without apology
Is the best that they gave to me.
My emotional strength gave a mighty pop.
Eventually I had to stop.
I stopped feeling things for years,
No more laughter, no more tears.
A phantom in a human's clothing;
No more love and no more loathing.
I wouldn't allow myself to feel,
Emptiness was all that was real.
Then suddenly I saw someone
Who looked like he was all undone.
His tired face, his shoulders slumped,
Looking like he'd just been thumped.
But he was not slinking away;
He helped another and made her day.
It wasn't great, his worn-out look,
But my numbness he truly shook.
A pitiful sight he was to see,
Yet he looked so beautiful to me.
The ice around my heart began

To melt the more I knew this man.
It took me quite by surprise,
The love I saw in his eyes,
Almost as much as what I felt.
My ice he continued to melt.
It took time for me to believe
That my heart had received a reprieve.
Once more I began to feel,
Emotions once again were real.
I'm so grateful for his heart's touch
For I have missed me so much.

TALK ABOUT THE WEATHER!

I shivered all winter,
The winds they were strong.
The rain was relentless,
The nights were so long.
The snow was too cold,
The hail too hard.
The kids couldn't even
Go play in the yard.

Fireplaces were causing
Smog all over town.
My neighbors weren't careful
And their house was burnt down!
The rattling of windows,
The crashing of thunder,
The yelping of dogs
'Neath the beds they hid under.

The sleet on the ground
And the frost from my breath;
The chest-ripping coughing
That sounded like death.
I just couldn't wait
For this winter to end,

For the sun to start shining,
For nature to mend.
Now summer is here
And I'm losing the plot.
Please bring back the winter.
It's too bloody hot!

LISTEN TO THE MUSIC

Listen to the music
In a child's laughter,
In a puppy's cute yelp,
Or a whine in a rafter.
There's a tune that plays
As cars drive past,
In rustling leaves,
Wind blowing fast.
A rhythmic beat
Is strong and loud
From clapping hands
Amongst a crowd.
A lively tempo
Fills the air
As kittens pounce
Around your chair.
The kitchen blender
Plays a song
With which the kettle
Whistles along.
The birds outside
Are joining in;
A bat hits a ball,
A boy kicks a tin.

Thunder crashes,
Rain hits the ground,
Hail falls with
A rat-a-tat sound.
A door slams shut,
And floorboards creak.
An apple is crunched,
And hungry mice squeak.
A sweet melody
Caresses your ear
As wind chimes chime
And sports fans cheer.
A young girl giggles,
A baby cries,
A lover whispers,
A mother sighs.
A telephone rings,
Some beetles chitter,
A twig is cracked
And butterflies flitter.
The world around you
Sings each night and day;
It's the song of life,
So listen to it play.

MONSTROUS HEATWAVE

While humans all hide with their air-con and
drinks,
Keeping their cool and their comfort complete,
The creatures and monsters throughout all the
land
Are suffering from this unconscionable heat.
As the temperature passes a hundred and twenty
The witches begin to spontaneously combust.
Vampires hiding in their darkened lairs
Stand helplessly by as their mates turn to dust.

The zombies shambling throughout the town
Start melting into ghastly puddles of goo,
Whilst poltergeists become suddenly visible,
Looking much like giant flees bred in Peru!
The dragons are unable to breathe any fire
As this insane heat sucks their lungs quite dry.
And Reapers are heaving all over their victims,
Wishing that it were themselves who could die.

Leprechauns outdo each other with tantrums
As there are no rainbows to lead them to gold,
But the gold has all melted like cheap dime-store
chocolate,

And trickles up mountainsides searching for
cold.
As night falls the goblins are roaming the streets,
Not knowing the who or the why or the how;
Their memories have seeped and escaped from
their brains
And these horrors have turned into lost children
now.

Some wicked gods smirk as they witness the
chaos,
Enjoying the suffering they've helped to incur,
But they all laugh out loud at the sight of
werewolves
Lining up at the salon to wax off their fur!
Now maybe this happened and maybe it didn't;
Just maybe my brain has been fried by the heat,
But next time the temperature passes one-twenty
Be kind to the monsters you see out in the street.

BEAUTIFUL TO ME

When I call you beautiful
I do not mean your face,
Or the style of your hair,
Guitar fingers full of grace.
Your voice as sweet as honey
I could listen to all night.
Your smile that quite thrills me
And makes everything alright.

Your perfect nose and cheekbones.
Your lips that tempt me so.
Your hands which are so manly,
Their touch I'd love to know.
Those hypnotizing eyes of yours
Are the most amazing blue,
But none of these are causing me
To see such beauty in you.

As much as all of these combine
And bring me so much pleasure,
All these combined don't equal
The parts of you that I so treasure.
Prejudice and bigotry
You work hard to destroy.
You share your time with others

And bring many so much joy.

The goodness of your heart
And the depth of your bright mind,
How you inspire others
And the way you are so kind.
So, when I close my eyes, dear one,
It is these things that I see,
And this is why, with all my heart,
You are so beautiful to me.

OVERWHELMING LOVE

An overwhelming love sears itself into your
heart
The day your son is born and changes your life
forever.
You watch him grow and all you know is
challenged
As he teaches you to see the world through his
eyes.
He takes you places you never thought you'd go.
He leads you through a minefield of emotions
As he experiences falls and achievements,
Or challenges your authority,
Reminding you that fatherhood
Is one of life's greatest challenges,
Whilst also being one of its deepest delights.
But the thing that amazes you most is that
As he grows, so does your love for him,
Something you didn't realise was possible.

You look at the man he has become and
sometimes
See reflections of the best of yourself,
And you are humbled.
Sometimes he follows in your footsteps;
Other times he forges his own path;

But at all times he is your pride and joy,
The one you love so dearly and so deeply.
He is a man in his own right,
But he is still, and always will be,
Your beautiful little boy,
And that overwhelming love for him
Will abide forever.

RESTING ON YOUR LAURELS

While you're resting on your laurels
Someone's beat you past the post.
No one looks at old achievements;
Last week's win is now a ghost.
If you want to keep on winning,
Keep on moving at a run;
You will not progress too far
Relying on memories of what's done.

Yesterday is quickly fading;
Time moves on and so must you.
People don't want last month's triumphs;
There's a craving for what's new.
It doesn't matter what you're doing;
People want the here and now.
Whatever you did, no matter how well,
You must do it better somehow.

If you want to make some headway
Make the effort that's required.
Work at being more successful
Lest you find yourself retired.
What you did is in the past
And no one goes to last year's fairs.

While you're resting on your laurels
Someone else is earning theirs.

CAN I TRUST YOU?

I've been alone for many years,
Protected from the pain and tears.
To love anew creates new fears.
So, can I trust you?

Will you speak to me with honesty,
And interact with integrity?
Is kindness what you'll show to me?
Please, can I trust you?

In your life, what will be my part?
Would you keep me in your heart?
Will you stay faithful when apart?
Tell me, can I trust you?

I've had a broken heart before
Of suffering I'll want no more.
Where do you stand on that score?
Now, can I trust you?

I can't stand infidelity,
And that rule's for both you and me.
As partners we should equals be.
I want to give as well as take.
I will do all for your sake.

I don't want either heart to break.

The things I ask I'll also give.
Mutual trust is imperative.
This is how a love should live.
And so, my dear, can I trust you?

JUST ONCE

Please let my love make love to me
Just once before I die.
Give me cause to shed tears of joy
Just once, for I will cry.
This cancer that is killing me
Is not my greatest fear.
What kills is knowing I'll never hold
The one I hold so dear.

So many things I used to want,
But they don't matter now.
My desires have changed drastically
Throughout the years somehow.
The house, the car, the pot of gold
Now don't mean anything.
The man I love is all I want,
But I'm winter to his spring.

My phoenix was burned many times,
But somehow rose again.
She's pulled us both back to the sky,
Up from the ashes of pain.
Allow my phoenix to fly high
Just once before she's done;
And let my love make love to me

Just once before I'm gone.

HEATHERBRAE

The moon shone over Heatherbrae;
We Wee Folk stirred amongst the trees.
A stranger dared near us to stray,
Her scent brought to us on the breeze.

She wandered here and wandered there;
And gently touched a leaf or two.
She saw a tiny Wee one stare!
Then gave the bow to show she knew.

This stranger meant to do no harm;
Pleasure she took at seeing us.
Her sparkling eyes held kindly charm;
We knew we had no need to fuss.

She spied a Night Rose full in bloom;
She gently sniffed but touched it not
As if she knew that that were doom!
(To touch a Night Rose made it rot.)

Grand Mater Wee as ruler stands;
She saw the stranger showed respect
For life within the Wee Folk lands.
Her presence we would not reject.

I am Grand Mater's eldest child
So I was tasked to grandly greet
This stranger from the Greater Wild,
(But truth be told it was a treat.)

She acted with civility,
Behaving with a humble grace.
She showed signs of gentility
We rarely saw amongst her race.

She stayed until the midnight hour,
We shared what looked a mighty bite;
I worried that she might devour
All of our food! I was not right.

Within her bag there were two plums;
She took them out and gifted them
As thanks for being friendly chums.
This Giant really was a gem!

But just as she prepared to go
A bat flew in amongst our trees,
But she was scared of nought you know
And faced it without trembling knees.

Just like a bat our Giant squealed
And led the creature in this way
Across the Tar Land to a field
With taller trees, and made it stay!

She saved the day that night somehow
And spared we Wee a nasty end,
And gratefully, forever now,
We call that stranger our dear friend.

FINE

You didn't vote for this government
So you can't be blamed for the state the country
is in.
You didn't agree to their hiking up taxes
Or increasing their own salaries.
You never approved the decline in education
standards
Or the increased cost of living.
You're not responsible.
Fine.

You didn't say "Yes" to failing infrastructure,
Overcrowding in hospitals,
Or increased unemployment due to
Outsourcing to other countries,
So you weren't the cause of the problems.
Fine.

But did you just say that you don't like the
Opposition?
They're no better than the governing Party?
You didn't vote for them either?
Fine.

Not everyone votes for the major players;

There are many micro-parties
Who concentrate on single issues;
Plus there are the independent candidates.
You didn't vote for any of those either?
You didn't vote at all,
Even though voting is mandatory?
Fine.

Now, because you chose to ignore your legal
responsibility,
From the Australian Electoral Commission to
you,
Here is a $222
Fine.

SILENT PACT

Our relationship has changed much over the
years.
Once full of drama and chaos and tears,
Now we're more like cousins who rarely keep in
touch;
We care about each other, but only so much.

Yet once we were lovers, a long time ago;
To look at us now though you'd never know.
We're not really friends but both put on the act;
For our children and grandkids we made a silent
pact.

Leave the past in the past; it's been 27 years
now.
There's no need to drag up the why or the how.
There's no more complaining or getting upset;
We've now reached as good as it's ever gonna
get.

We no longer terrorise each other's mind
With hatred and blaming and being unkind.
In old age we're better than one might expect;
We've grown up now, showing each other
respect.

INTO THE FIRE

I threw myself into the fire,
But instead of burning
I found myself cleansed.

The utter freedom
Of baring my soul
Has proven to be a soothing balm.

I accept that I can't have
Everything or everyone
That I want in this life.

Yet still, I insist that
I keep striving towards
A better life for myself.

What can't I do now,
Now that I'm able to speak the truth
And bear the consequences?

Life begins on the day
You decide to start living it,
And today will do just fine.

After awakening from
An emotional numbness,
I feel as if I have been reborn.

During the years which had passed for a life,
I had been thrown into the fire
And I was charred.

I was burned at the stake as a witch;
I was sacrificed on the alter
Of the desires of devils.

I was stomped on, spat at,
Pushed into the mud;
But no more the victim, I.

I have chosen a new path for myself,
One seeking happiness through
Self-acceptance and accountability.

I threw myself into the fire
And arose from the ashes,
A phoenix, ready to fly.

I AM MY OWN RAINBOW

Red is the blood running through my veins,
The river of life that flows within me,
From my first moment until my very last.

Orange is the flame of love, passion, excitement,
Drive and ambition that sets my soul on fire,
And encourages my blood to keep on pumping.

Yellow is the sun beneath which I bask,
Play, labour, stumble, love, lose, and hope,
Rising again each day, urging me to do the same.

Green is the grass, the foliage on bushes and
trees,
New life sprouting all around come rain or
shine,
As a reminder that even in sorrowful times life
goes on.

Blue is the colour of my eyes
That witness the beauty all around me,
And seek out the goodness and love in people.

Indigo is the midnight sky,
Watching over me while I sleep or when I can't,

Protecting me and my ego from constant
brightness.

Violet is the colour of luxury,
The greatest of which is being a free citizen,
Well educated and being permitted to think for
myself.

I am my own rainbow, weathering life's storms.
My pot of gold will never be in having had a
perfect life,
But in knowing that I at least tried to make it a
better one.